The Sales Superstar Bible

EVERYTHING YOU NEED TO KNOW TO BE THE TOP PRODUCING SALES PROFESSIONAL IN YOUR COMPANY

MICHAEL LEPPO

PRESIDENT

STRATEGIC SALES CLOSERS

Published by
Strategic Sales Closers LLC
10 Dustin Drive, Lawrenceville, NJ. 08648

ISBN: 0-9765752-0-5

Library of Congress Cataloging –in-Publication Data
Leppo, Michael
The Superstars Sales Bible (Everything You Need To Know To Be The Top Producing Sales Professional In Your Company)
Michael Leppo – 1st ed.

This publication is designed to provide accurate and authoritative information with regard to the subject matter covered. It is sold with the understanding that the publisher is not engaged in rendering legal, accounting, or other professional advice. If legal advice or other expert assistance is required, the services of a competent professional person should be sought. From a Declaration of Principles jointly adopted by a committee of the American Bar Association and a Committee of Publishers and Associations.

This book is available at quantity discounts for bulk purchases (see page 93).

Visit our homepage at http://www.strategicsalesclosers.com

I dedicate this book to my wife, Tamara.
You are the love of my life, my passion, and best friend.
Thank you for your support.

CONTENTS

INTRODUCTION

In my opinion, this is the greatest sales book ever written. This book uses more than twenty years of quota-busting sales experience and presents this knowledge in an easy-to-read compact version of what Sales Superstars do in order to achieve greatness. This book will help all sales professionals, whether you are a brand new sales professional or a seasoned veteran. It is my goal to turn you into a Superstar Sales Professional. In order to do this, you must invest your time and energy on a consistent basis on the following: practice and rehearse your presentations, anticipate and overcome objections, and countless other important things which you will find within the pages of this book.

The art of selling is a profession just like being a doctor, attorney, or accountant. Unfortunately, average sales people treat being in sales with little respect. Some just "wing it," which does the greatest disservice to them individually as well as to the profession itself. By "winging it," some sales people cheat themselves out of being the best they can be and cheat themselves out of numerous sales that, with preparation and knowledge, could have rewarded them time and time again.

The steps that follow are proven, work very well and will help you to stay on track as you begin or further your sales career. Use this book daily to remind yourself of the basics and principles you need to apply to help you achieve greatness. This book was designed as a quick reference primer and is part of the Strategic Sales Closers Self Improvement Series.

Refer to this book as a constant reminder of how to succeed. The author has a lifetime sales achievement record of averaging over 500% of quota selling over 100 products and services ranging in values from $1,000 to $5M during the past 20 years. The words that follow will help make you the top producing sales professional in your company. It is up to you to turn words into action and make it happen.

Enjoy,

Michael Leppo

President

Strategic Sales Closers

www.strategicsalesclosers.com

Key Traits of Superstars

CHAPTER ONE

We will explore all the traits, characteristics, strategies, and intangibles that Superstar Sales Performers have in common. For the purposes of this book we will define a Superstar Sales Professional as someone who is able to achieve 150% of his or her given quota for five consecutive years. This not only will make you a Sales Superstar but will also make you very wealthy. So let's get started.

Let's begin by listing some of the key characteristics of Sales Superstars. This list is not all-inclusive but rather provides some common traits that superstars have. Refer to this list often to see where and how you are measuring up. There is always room for improvement and fine-tuning. Let this list be one compass.

THE 25 TRAITS OF A SUPERSTAR SALES PROFESSIONAL

1. **Project a Positive Mental Attitude** - Sales Superstars show that they are positive, certain, and confident. If not, their prospects would not believe in them.

2. **Are Highly Disciplined Especially With Their Time** – They are extremely disciplined in many areas. Their time management may be their strongest discipline. Superstars use time as an ally not an enemy. Internally, they use time to organize their day and make their daily strategic plan. Externally, time is used to get their prospects to take action. Your time is something you have 100% control over. Use it wisely and your sales numbers could be staggering. Use it poorly and you

could find yourself looking for another profession.

3. ***Sales Superstars Do Creative Preparation*** – They think "out of the box." We will spend a lot of time discussing this vital key to success; sales superstars do things others have not even considered.

4. ***They Constantly Create New Power Questions*** – Tools. Every profession has them. Superstar Sales Professionals' tools are highly developed questions.

5. ***They Listen Attentively*** – This may be the most important tool in the bag. Sales Superstars listen actively and ask questions based on what the prospect JUST SAID! They don't wait anxiously for THEIR turn to talk simply to ask a litany of questions. Poor, non-active listening will lose you more sales than anything else you do.

6. ***Sales Superstars Do Not Compromise When It Comes To Providing Quality Service*** – You must, I repeat, must provide your clients with service that is not only excellent but consistently superior to any other vendor they work with. Extensive studies have been done on customer loyalty and satisfaction. Just because your customers say they are satisfied does not mean they will be loyal.

7. ***Sales Superstars Always Sell To The Customers' Needs*** – As a Sales Superstar, you are truly in the Customer Needs business. Customers will always have wants and desires which need to be met. By asking proper questions, you can easily uncover most of these. Then, your product and service can be described in terms that will

meet these needs. In 99% of the cases you must meet and exceed the customers' needs if you want their business.

8. **Sales Superstars Prospect And Qualify For Money And Budget** – How aggravated have you become when you have invested your time and money in planning a trip that turns out to be a disaster (the beach or pool is closed, the food is horrible, the place is not kid friendly, or not romantic enough for the special event)? It is highly probable that you did a poor job asking the kinds of questions that would have led you to understand exactly what you were heading into. Your poor qualifying yielded you a less than idyllic experience.

    Qualifying your business prospects is NOT any different, is it? If you invest your time, money, and energy in prospects that do not have an interest in, or enough money to buy your product, or if their time frame is a few years out, then you experience the same aggravation and frustration you experienced when you made your personal arrangements.

    Your time is too important to be spent with non-qualified or poor prospects. **YOU MUST BECOME AN EXCELLENT QUALIFIER IN ORDER TO BECOME A SUPERSTAR!**

9. **Sales Superstars Network Where The Prospects Are** – Make sure you invest your time in proper places. Do not join your local Chamber of Commerce if you see no possible return on your investment. Network with others who can help you and vice versa. **Networking in the wrong places will use up your most valuable resource: Time.**

10. ***Sales Superstars Have An Intense Desire To Succeed*** – Find a way to motivate yourself to become great if you are not already great. Your passion for what you are doing and your desire to be a success (whether financially or achieving top ranking each month) will ultimately be a major deciding factor in whether or not you will succeed.

11. ***Sales Superstars Believe Honesty And Trust Cannot Be Compromised*** – Sales superstars are typically of very strong moral and ethical fiber. There are exceptions to this, and you have likely come across people who fit the bill. These are NOT true Sales Superstars and, more likely than not, their staying power was short-lived. Honesty and truth never go out of style: the rewards come back many times over.

12. ***Sales Superstars Have Total Conviction In Themselves And In Their Product Or Service*** – Have you bought anything from people who use words like *"could, might, let's see if it works"*? Of course not! Sales Superstars have total conviction and belief in what they do. The belief is so strong, that the excitement is transferred to prospects almost magically. Your words, eyes, body language, and resolve are major factors in winning or losing deals.

13. ***Sales Superstars Are Service Oriented*** – Superstars genuinely care about their customers and therefore make sure they are happy. It is as simple as that.

14. ***Sales Superstars Manage Their Time Very Effectively*** – See #2. A Sales Superstar understands that proper time management is 100% critical to their success. Here is

a perfect example.

Many years ago I worked as a stockbroker for a large Wire House in Massachusetts. During my employment I worked regular 80-hour weeks in which I was on the phone dialing for dollars about 96% of time. When I was not dialing, I was preparing to dial or meeting with clients. I managed to produce excellent numbers for a first-year broker. Sitting close by my work area were three older people who were just starting out in the business as well. I thought that I should watch and listen to what they did since they were older and probably more knowledgeable than I. Wrong! These three brokers played on the Quotetron (Stock Ticker) all day. They researched companies all day but never called anyone. Guess what? No one ever called them either. They had the lowest production of anyone in the firm. Zero dollars in production is hardly producing! All three were let go after six months.

DO NOT CONFUSE YOUR ROLE. IF YOU ARE A SALES PERSON THEN YOU NEED TO SELL! YOU DO NOT NEED TO BECOME YOUR COMPANY'S RESEARCH ANALYST.

15. *Sales Superstars Possess Positive Mental Preparation Skills* – You MUST PREPARE for each and every meeting or presentation as if it were your very first or very last presentation ever. Remember, your prospects do not know that you totally blew it on your last sales call or that you have not made a sale in three months.

Prepare as if this meeting is the most important meeting of your life; it could be! And prepare with the mind set that you ARE the highly confident sales superstar that you imagine yourself to be.

16. ***Sales Superstars Are Masters Of Product Knowledge*** – In this day of specialization you must be an expert in what you do. The only way to become an expert is to put in the hours learning. There is no excuse for lack of product knowledge. You are your product. The knowledge you possess will establish you as an expert or consultant with your product and most importantly in the eyes of the prospect.

Make sure you hit the books or the Internet. There is no excuse for not doing this!

17. ***Sales Superstars Understand The Psychology Of Themselves And Their Prospects / Clients*** – You must become a master of what your prospects are thinking. This is one of those intangible skills that is usually developed over a period of time. Your experience will go a long way in helping you close sales others would not or could not simply because you understand yourself and your prospect better than the competition does.

18. ***Sales Superstars Are Consistent In Their Daily Activities*** – Superstars have a detailed, specific plan <u>every</u> day and indeed have a short-, medium- and long-term plans. These plans analyze in detail their ideas and strategies over a period of time. The daily, detailed plan provides step-by-step details with time limits and goals used to achieve the short, medium and long-range plans. Every person works differently but it is crucial to lay the framework of the plan…its goals, its action steps, every step necessary to get to achieve the ultimate plan. Also to work the plan, you must understand what makes you tick. You must know when during the day you are most effective and when during the day you are most ineffective. Use this to your advantage.

As an example: The best time of day for me to speak to or meet with prospects and clients is from 7 A.M. – 2 P.M. This is my peak time, my most energetic and focused time of day. Therefore, I consistently do the bulk of my phone and in-person meetings during those hours. I leave the administrative or busy work for all other hours. During these "off" hours I tend to be more sluggish. This understanding of myself allows me to be more consistent and more productive on a daily basis.

You need to understand yourself so you can be your best.

19. ***Sales Superstars Always Have A List Of Reasons Why Their Prospects Should Invest In Their Product Or Service*** – A superstar is always, **always** ready to talk to prospects about the benefits of their product or service. You need to be able to roll out of bed and hit the pavement running. This means you live and breathe your product or service. You must be able to talk the talk at any given moment whether you are faced with a two-minute elevator pitch or in talking between golf shots.

Master the benefits of your product or service and make them your own.

20. ***Sales Superstars Read Business And Selling Books On A Regular Basis*** – Other professionals (doctors, dentists, psychologists) regularly attend seminars, read books, publish articles, and attend trade shows. Similarly, Sales Superstars are masters of their product, masters of the industry they work in, and masters in the profession of selling. They too read pertinent books and articles, attend training seminars and speak to other master sales professionals to compare notes and to get ideas.

21. ***Typically, Sales Superstars Are Nice People*** – The fact is that most very successful sales professionals are good people. There are many who are bastards but these people typically do not have lasting success in business or in their personal lives. It pays to be a good person. You can sleep well at night and look back on your career at various stages and be proud of the work you have done.

22. ***Sales Superstars Have A Customer Appreciation Day On A Monthly Basis*** – This is something I started years ago. This is a regular part of my schedule. About every four to six weeks I contact my current clients to make sure all is well. Typically this yields additional business either from my clients or business in the form of referrals.

If this doesn't seem like something you are comfortable with then hear this: be certain that your competition is talking to them at least monthly and trying to steal them at every given moment.

Never ever take your client's business or loyalty for granted. It can disappear in a heartbeat.

23. ***Sales Superstars Know When To Get Away From Their Job*** – Superstars are smart enough to know when to rest and get away from their business. Find ways to energize and revitalize yourself along the way. On a large scale, I reward myself by going away on vacations. Vacations energize and revitalize me and generally help me to stay motivated, fresh, and upbeat. While this may not be practical every week, there are things you can do to reward yourself even daily. Some examples: Take a walk, play some sports, treat yourself to a great bottle of wine, or end 'early' for the day following a job well done, go for a massage. What kinds of things energize you? What are your rewards?

Find ways to keep yourself energized and rewarded for a job well done.

24. ***Sales Superstars Understand Their Clients' Needs Very Well*** – Needless to say, you must become a master of who your client or prospect is. Know what is happening in the industry or within their company. Are your contacts motivated financially to doing business with you? Is that person's job on the line if things fail? Is your client's company losing money to a new or existing competitor? Is your contact the right person to talk to and is he/she the final decision maker? Who is the final decision maker?

Superstars have their thumb on the pulse of what is of significance to their prospects and clients.

25. ***Sales Superstars Are Master Qualifiers*** – When writing a sales book it is difficult to state what the most important ingredient to becoming and maintaining superstar status is exactly. Qualifying well is without a shadow of a doubt one of the most important skills a superstar exhibits. How many times have you driven a considerable distance to meet with a prospect who turned out to be dud?

My guess is that this has happened to you a few times. Before leaving your office you must qualify your prospects so well that you know virtually everything about them before you see them. You might ask "What is the purpose of having a meeting if I already have asked them all my questions"?

This is an excellent question. The reasons you ask numerous questions on the phone are the following:

1. So you know with 99% certainty if this is truly a well-qualified prospect.

2. So you can prepare like a professional for the meeting. This means knowing not only what products or services to present but also what intangibles will probably arise during the meeting. For instance if the prospect has been well qualified then you should know what type of person you will be meeting. The type of person is determined by both his/her title but also by personality type.

Understanding the personality type is crucial. If you have prepared a long-winded presentation and are meeting with a difficult, combative, time-is-money executive, then you are going to have trouble.

Years ago I had a meeting with one of the largest Financial Services companies in the world. It took me more than 14 months to get the meeting and was told that the meeting would take place from 1 to 4 P.M. I would be meeting with 12-15 senior executives. Along with me were four consultants who were not sales professionals. They were, however, extremely knowledgeable about our service both technically and from an industry knowledge standpoint.

Over a four-week period I prepared the consultants and myself for what we expected would be a very involved three-hour meeting. On the day of the meeting we arrived thirty minutes early to set up laptops, monitors and assorted graphs, and charts. Guess what happened?

Our host decided to show up thirty minutes *late* to

the meeting which was taking place in his own building. Then they said *"Show us what you have. You've got thirty minutes"*! I thought, "Thirty minutes? Are you out of your mind? How the hell are we going to get through a 75-page PowerPoint presentation in which each consultant is scheduled to speak for at least 25 minutes?

Well, as a credit to the intense preparation and understanding of my prospect's needs and wants as well as a thorough knowledge of exactly what made them tick, we were successful. During the thirty-minute meeting I took charge and immediately cut out the extraneous material and tightly focused on the prospect and the people in the room. My consultants barely got a word in because it was not needed. What was more important was that we let our rude hosts speak and that we responded accordingly. What transpired was selling excellence at its best. In the end, we landed a very significant sale.

CHAPTER TWO

POSITIVE MENTAL ATTITUDE

"People can alter their lives by altering attitudes".
—William James

Your attitude affects everything you do. It affects how people perceive you, it affects your health and it even affects your success in life. Developing and maintaining a positive mental attitude is one of the most crucial intangibles you can have as a Sales Superstar.

I play a game with myself all the time that proves my point. When I go out to do the normal errands we all do (going to the dry cleaners, the Jiffy Lube, mechanic, or the grocery store) I carefully observe the person waiting on me to see how they act. Most of the time the people providing service are making minimum wage. Typically, these workers have poor attitudes and provide poor service. I can't say I blame them. But the attitude they project toward me and others is what they get in return. Doesn't it make sense that they should at least pretend to be enjoying themselves? Almost 100% of the time the workers who are friendly receive friendly comments and typically sell more of their services or products than do the sullen, angry workers whom we all have to deal with.

It is very interesting. You can tell a lot about a person just by watching their mannerisms and body language: the look in their eyes, the way they stand, their physical appearance, whether they make eye contact or look away. All of these factors are the direct reflection of attitude. If they rate highly in the above categories, they are likely to have an excellent attitude.

Watch out for people with poor attitudes. If the people providing you service possess a poor attitude notice how your own behavior changes. It can't help but affect you in a negative way. Negativity, bitterness and sour faces spread like wildfire and creep in when you least expect it. Check your attitude from time to time to make sure you have not been infected with this insidious poison.

Superstars stay positive no matter who or what is thrown at them. As a sales professional you can pretty much set your watch by a few things: Management will raise your quota every year but tell you that under this new plan you will make more money; your company's new product or service will have some serious kinks or flaws in it but you will still be asked to sell it regardless; your competition will steal one of your prized clients; you will have days where absolutely nothing goes right.

What you need to ask or think about every time you find yourself in this position is "*So What*"? Put off taking any drastic action until you sleep on what is weighing on your mind. You can avoid so much stress and heartache by asking the simple words "So What?" and dealing with it freshly in the morning. Usually the crisis can be resolved in a much better way.

No matter what, Sales Superstars do not let problems that they have no control over affect their attitude or behavior. Life is too short. Stay positive and focused on what you can do or what you can change.

SOME WAYS SALES SUPERSTARS DEVELOP AND MAINTAIN A POSITIVE MENTAL ATTITUDE:

1. **Smile** – Try this as you are reading and see how you feel. Smiling makes you feel light and lessens the stress you are under. Smiling makes you feel better. Smiling is the number one key to developing and maintaining a positive outlook.

2. **Stay away from negativity** – Negativity is a disease that can wear you down and destroy your hopes and dreams. Years ago I worked for a company as an outside sales representative. From time to time I had to go in to the office. It always amazed me that as soon as I walked into the office other sales representatives would come out of the woodwork to talk to me about all that was wrong with the company, the management, the new compensation plan, how the competition had a new and better product, how they should have been given a promotion. Sound familiar?

    What did I do? I always had a focused plan when entering the office. The plan was directly proportional to the amount of money I put in the parking meter. I made sure that I was in and out of the office within 25-45 minutes and had absolutely no extra time to talk about anything other than closing business. There were five salespeople who worked in that office. One year I out-produced all five combined.

A POSITIVE ATTITUDE IS AN ALL-THE-TIME TRAIT; NOT JUST SOMETHING TO HAVE WHEN IT IS CONVENIENT.

3. Avoid bad influences – Daily, bad influences are all around us. Bad influences can take many shapes and forms such as: negative people, negative management, watching too much television, over-eating, not exercising, smoking, or drinking too much.

A Sales Superstar recognizes when these forces creep in to his/her world. A Sales Superstar takes control over every facet so these bad influences do not pull him/her down in any way.

4. Sales Superstars learn how to embrace failure and disappointment – That's right. Sales superstars realize quickly that life is not fair. There will be minor and major disappointments along the way. This realization makes them strong. Learn from your failures so you don't repeat the same mistakes.

Have you ever lost a big sale? It is impossible for you to be a top performing sales professional unless you have lost numerous big sales. Why? These experiences are what teach you to get better, to become more observant, to get more organized, to be more emphatic, and to become a much better Sales Superstar.

Sales Superstars understand that they will lose on occasion. This knowledge and a strong dislike of losing is what drives them to become the best they can be each and every time and ultimately, become more successful.

5. ***Compliment and listen to others*** – This simple step will put you in the proper frame of mind daily. Your positive actions toward others will make you feel better and will cause others to look upon you more favorably. These positive actions will lead to more positive emotions in you and lead to a more positive attitude.

It is important to show that a positive mental attitude is more than just some fancy way of saying 'be a good person'. I have listed below some examples of some famous people who have positive attitudes. These observations were made while watching these people interact during interviews or in other social situations.

1. Muhammad Ali – Known as the greatest. Ali transcends the sports world because of his incredibly charismatic positive energy and attitude. He is one of the most recognizable and beloved figures in the world. Ali always smiles and jokes in spite of his illness. He is great because he is able to make others feel special and good. His is a rare gift, and is truly one of the most positive uplifting figures of all time.

2.Mike Eruzione – Former captain of the 1980 "Miracle on Ice" US Hockey Team. They beat the Russians and won the Gold Medal. Eruzione's passion and enthusiasm were then, and remain today, very inspiring. He captured America's heart with his determination and selfless acts of teamwork. His insistence that ALL his teammates join him on the gold medal podium is one of my favorite moments ever in sports.
    Eruzione has made an excellent living following his game winning goal and as a result of his enthusiasm. His

positive energy is living proof that passion and positive attitude can yield major results.

3. Oprah Winfrey – Oprah is the epitome of the words passion, enthusiasm, and zest for life. Think for a moment: Is Oprah a great interviewer? Is she a great listener? Is she very attractive? It doesn't really matter. The fact is that Oprah's zest for life is contagious and that is why she is one of the wealthiest and most successful people in the world.

Your positive attitude will open more doors for you than anything else in life.

CHAPTER THREE

CONFIDENCE AND CONVICTION

You must have Confidence and Conviction if you ever hope to achieve greatness. Right now, as I write this book, President George W. Bush is under great pressure and scrutiny for his decision to invade Iraq. President Bush has been second-guessed by virtually every one but he maintains tremendous conviction in his decision. This conviction is what makes him appealing to many people. He portrays a confident, sure-of-himself manner and shows no sign of weakness or doubt when speaking about his decision to invade Iraq. Despite intense questioning and protests, he holds his ground firm and in turn makes his prospects (that is, potential voters/buyers of his service) comfortable.

You must have the same conviction in the actions you take regardless of the outcome. Your conviction must be clear and strong in your voice as you speak with potential clients. Your conviction is what sells. The moment you begin second-guessing yourself or management or the product/service you are selling, then your numbers will go down significantly. Your prospects will sense your lack of confidence. This intangible trait will cause you to fail.

The question: *"How do I come across as confident and convincing if I am new to sales or my numbers are poor?"* There are many ways to accomplish this. Every morning when you wake up and every evening before you go to sleep look in the mirror and repeat the following: *"I am the top producing sales person in my company"*. Repeat this ten times, slowly, each time with more passion and conviction. Notice what happens to your posture, your voice, your facial expression each time you say these words.

You will start to notice almost magically a change in your demeanor and confidence. This is the very first step to becoming a superstar.

Why Do This?

Simply, it works.

I do this because of my own personal experience. It happened to me when I was 21 years old.

When I was 21 years old I was working as a stockbroker for a major brokerage firm in Massachusetts. In my first ten months in the business I had made about $14,000. I was working 80 hours a week cold calling between 300 and 400 people daily. I was working like a dog.

One evening after another 300+ rejections I went for a drink with a co-worker "Scott". Scott was the #1 producing stockbroker in the office. He was 24 years old and was making close to $20,000 a month. Scott was about five feet five inches tall, more than one half foot shorter than I am. During the evening we started talking about business and that's when my sales career and my life changed forever.

Without even realizing what I was saying, I must have said once too-many times, "*Well I'm only 21*". Scott grabbed me by the collar and started yelling at me like I have never been yelled at before. He practically screamed, "*You keep saying you are only 21 years old and that's what is coming across on the phone. Prospects are not going to give their money to some 21 year old kid. From this moment forward you are 35 years old and you are the number one producing stockbroker in the office. You don't have time for small prospects. Do you hear me?!*".

I did not know what to do. I thought about punching him but decided against it. Then I drove home and could not get to sleep. How the hell am I supposed to be 35 years old when I am only 21 and how the hell am I the #1 producing sales person when I am barely making $1,200 month?

Over the next day or two I listened to Scott speak to prospects. I could hear the difference in his voice. I knew that he knew what he was talking about. Hell, I was ready to give him MY money by the time he hung up the phone. After that I saw how easy it was...an acting game, really. I convinced myself that I was 35 years old and, yes, I was the #1 producer in the office. All my actions, my mannerisms, and demeanor reflected this new person. The results were absolutely astonishing. Over the next thirty days I became one of the top-producing stockbrokers in the office. I closed 35 new accounts for the month (anyone who is in the business will tell you this is phenomenal). I was the #3 highest grossing broker for the month, and earned $14,500. I made more that month than I had earned the entire year before. And that was only the beginning.

You can change your career and sales numbers just by doing the above. You have complete control over your attitude and you can become whomever you want to be. You just need to put your mind to it and believe it!

CHAPTER FOUR

DESIRE, PASSION, AND ENTHUSIASM

Desire – def. A wanting or longing; strong wish.

Nothing stops the man who desires to achieve.
Every obstacle is simply a course to
develop his achievement muscle.
It's a strengthening of his powers of accomplishments.
—Eric Butterworth

As we discussed in the last chapter, your desire is what will catapult you forward or hold you back. Below are some questions that will help you gauge your current level of desire. The answers may shock you.

What are my desires?

1. What do I need to do to become #1? Do I have a plan and a clear vision? If yes, what is that plan?
2. How many calls do I need to make in order to achieve my daily/monthly goal?
3. What are my strengths?
4. What are my weaknesses?
5. What am I willing to sacrifice to become #1 in the office?
6. What type of enthusiasm do I have for my product or service? How do others view me? Happy, energetic, dull, not intelligent, not credible?

The answers to these questions will provide important information about you and your abilities. If you do not have answers to these questions then it probably tells you that your desire for greatness is not as great as you thought it was. Superstars know the answers to these questions. They work on these questions and goals daily.

Chapter Five

Passion – def. Strong feeling or emotion

In my life, I define passion as something I love so much that doing it is the greatest thing in the world; it is effortless, easy. I always have energy and time to spend on it. My passion is my children. No matter how tired I am I want to be with my children.

Professionally, I am passionate about anything and everything having to do with selling. I enjoy speaking about selling, I love training sales professionals, and writing about it. I know that I am the greatest sales professional in the world. This is not because I have a track record of over 500% of quota in many industries selling many different products and services. I know that I am the greatest because I can sell anything to anyone. I thoroughly understand the nuances and flow of sales and I am passionate about the process.

- **Very simply: Are you passionate about what you do?**
- **Do you believe 100% in your product or service?**
- **Do you find 100% joy in what you are doing?**
- **Are you 100% passionate in your occupation and cannot wait to wake up every morning ready to get at it?**
- **Do you desire to improve and be better than you are today?**

If you answered yes, then you are on the right path to becoming a superstar. If you answered no, then I suggest that you choose a different occupation.

Working hard will yield good results; passion will make you a superstar.

Chapter Six

Enthusiasm – def. Eager interest, zeal

Ok. You have a strong desire and passion to succeed. But do you come across as enthusiastic or dull as a door-knob? Regardless of your personality, you must find a way to show your prospects that you enthusiastically want to work with them and that there is nowhere in the world you would rather be.

At the same time, you need to temper your enthusiasm so that you do not come across inappropriately. For instance, if your prospect is really soft spoken and dull, then unbridled enthusiasm is not the way to go. Match your prospect's personality but maintain appropriate enthusiasm at all times.

Enthusiasm sells. Just look at Oprah, Mary Lou Retton, or Richard Simmons. These people are all highly successful and highly enthusiastic about what they are doing.

CHAPTER SEVEN

Persistence – A persisting; stubborn continuance.
Resoluteness, endurance.

Persistence is a valuable tool that you carry. The reality of selling is that no matter how great your product or service is, you still need to makes numerous calls and have many meetings to close the deal. Sometimes you may call someone 20 times before they tell you that they are not interested.

Your ability to stay persistent regardless of the obstacles in your way will determine your greatness.

Ray Kroc of MacDonald's had a nice way of looking at persistence. Listed below is his view:

PERSISTENCE

Nothing can take the place of persistence
Threat will not
Nothing is more common
Than the unsuccessful men
With great talent
Genius will not
Unheralded genius is almost a proverb
Education will not
The world is full of
Educated derelicts
Persistence and
Determination
Alone are omnipotent.

Preparation and Beliefs

CHAPTER EIGHT

Objections – def. a reason or argument presented in opposition; a feeling or expression of disapproval

Life is one big objection. No matter what you do in life you will get objections from someone. No one ever agrees 100% with what you have to say. If this is the case, why do most sales reps get so worried about objections? Why are more sales lost when objections arise than at any other time in the sales process?

There are a number of reasons but first let's put objections in perspective. First of all you have to be a complete idiot not to expect objections during the sales process. Secondly, certain objections show that your prospect is interested. This means objections are really opportunities dressed in disguise.

Opportunities Dressed in Disguise: I have never understood why some sales professionals get nervous about objections. The primary reason this happens is because they were not properly prepared. So what is "proper preparation"?

The more a sales professional is prepared for a meeting the better he/she is able to handle any objection that may arise. The fact is, you should be able to *predict* what your prospect is going to object to or what issues will be raised. So how do you handle the objection?

There are two ways to handle an objection. *The first way is to raise the objection yourself! This is by far the most effective way to handle it!* That's right, if you raise the objection first, then you can present the objection in your terms and in terms the prospect will not find objectionable.

For example, if you know your prospect loves his/her current vendor and has no interest in switching, what would you do? During the course of your questions you should ask the prospect about his/her current vendor and learn everything about the vendor— the good, the bad, and the neutral. Then, use this information to discuss the merits of your own company and its services as it relates to the customer's needs. The reality is that the prospect may not really be thrilled with the vendor but really just doesn't want to make a change of any kind and so remain status quo.

Your job is to ask leading questions initially that help you gather useful information so you can overcome these objections without their being raised. If you do this effectively, you will be viewed as a trusted consultant versus a backpedaling sales person.

The second way of handling objections is to answer them as they come. You have no choice in the matter. The way these objections are answered is always with a question. A well-used example is, "Does it come in red?" And you reply "If I could get it in red for you, do we have a deal?" This example is a clear and simple demonstration of overcoming a possible objection

You should always answer the objection with a question. By asking the question you are able to dig a little deeper and find out if the prospect has a legitimate objection, a condition, or just a misunderstanding. The reality is that the objection might just be a smokescreen and not be of any significance to the prospect. In fact, he/she is WAITING for you to ask more about the objection that was just raised. This helps to define and get very clear about what exactly the REAL objection is.

The bottom line is that the more prepared you are, the more likely you will be able to predict what questions and objections your prospects will have. Being well prepared and asking the right questions will allow you to take charge of the situation. This will create a higher likelihood of success.

CHAPTER NINE

SHUT UP AND LISTEN!

As a professional sales superstar, it is critical that you gather information. The only way to do that well is to listen. The more you talk the more you sound like a "Salesperson" and the more likely you will lose in the long run. Conversely, the more the prospect talks, the more likely you will win in the long run. People love the sound of their own voice, so let them talk. It is ironic but true: the more the prospect talks, the more he/she likes you and your product or service.

The most common phrase you will hear your sales manager use when describing the approach above is "Consultative Selling". This is a fancy phrase to describe a selling style in which you ask intelligent questions and listen to your prospect. In other words, ask questions and then shut up. A great rule of thumb is: if you are talking more than the prospect, then you are being perceived as a "Salesperson" and will NOT get the sale. If you find that the prospect is talking more than you are, then you are probably being perceived as a consultant and have a much better chance of winning the sale.

CHAPTER 10

PREPARE, PREPARE, PREPARE!

Don't be nervous,
Don't be flustered,
Don't be scared;
Be prepared
—Boy Scout's Marching Song, by Tom Lehrer.

You can never be too prepared, too well-dressed, look too well groomed, be in too good shape, have too good manners....You get the picture.

Preparation is one of the most critical steps to Superstar Selling. Being well prepared separates the average sales performer from the Sales Superstar. Total preparation means you go in to each sales call (whether by phone, by email, by letter, or face-to-face) with as much knowledge of every possible issue or angle that could be raised during your meeting. Some issues could be competitive, the company's background and your own company's background, political situation of the people you are meeting (did they recently hire a new CEO or did their former CFO become involved in an audit scandal, and so on).

You must be willing to take this extra step. Your competitors are doing it. If you do not prepare well, then decide right now that you will always be average. There is no excuse for not being prepared or for not having the appropriate information when you exit a meeting. You may ask, *"How do I prepare: What should I use to prepare for the meeting?"* Excellent questions with very simple answers.

The Internet is by far the greatest tool the Sales Superstar has available. Here, anyone can gather every possible piece of information on almost any company, industry, prospect's competitors, even your prospects themselves (depending on their visibility in the community or company). You will find breaking news, in-depth studies and/or commentaries on industry concerns that occur moments before your meeting. The Internet is always up-to-date. Some of the information you should be looking for includes: Financial reports, current and historical news, company press releases (both current and dated), information about the prospect's competition and your own company's competition, and biographies or quotations of some of the people you will be meeting with.

It is extremely important that you learn to invest your time wisely and prepare appropriately for every call in the sales process. In other words, do not spend three hours preparing for every cold call if you need to make 300 calls to make one sale. Conversely, it may make complete sense to prepare for a week if you are selling $5M+ worth of product or service to a company.

Prepare, prepare, and prepare some more. Also, use the internet and any personal friends or associates who may help you prepare for success.

CHAPTER 11

UNDERSTAND THY PRODUCT OR SERVICE

Pretty basic statement, isn't it? The question is: How can you ever hope to make a sale if you do not know what you are talking about? Study your product or service. Use it, buy it (if appropriate), practice with it. Understand its uses, strengths, and weaknesses. Understand how it can be used by your prospect and why it will save them money and make them more efficient.

Zig Ziglar was one of the great sales trainers of all time. Zig started out selling cookware door-to-door many years ago. He struggled mightily but kept working. Zig was unsuccessful early because he didn't truly believe in the product. He thought he did, but truly he did not...and it showed! The cookware he was selling cost over $1,000 which was very expensive. Zig was having trouble convincing prospects to spend $1,000. Why? Because Zig had not invested $1,000 in the cookware himself.

After he finally invested in his own cookware his sales went through the roof. Why?

As a sales professional you need to believe with every fiber of your body that what you are selling is the latest and greatest product or service on the market. Until you do, your prospects will see right through you. To paraphrase Zig: You gotta buy the cookware to believe in the cookware.

CHAPTER 12

BELIEVE IN YOUR PRODUCT.
IF YOU DON'T, NO ONE ELSE WILL

This is another step in the process that could very well be the most important key to successful selling. Your belief, passion, and enthusiasm will become apparent to anyone you meet very quickly just as your lack of these traits will come through too. Words are words and they are empty and meaningless unless each word and phrase is delivered from your lips to the prospect's ears with passion. Prospects can hear (and you can feel) when your heart is truly in it....when you are speaking with conviction and power. These are the intangible clues that exude confidence and control. This passion, this power and confidence set your prospects at ease...they feel comfortable in your presence and in turn feel comfortable with you and your solution. Find your power, your belief, your passion.

You must truly believe in your product or service. If you do not believe in your product/service then find something else to do. To reiterate: your belief in your product or service is what will make you a Sales Superstar or not. I know from personal experience. When I fully invested all my belief, my mind and my soul, the results were sales numbers that were of historic significance. During the time that I was just going through the motions, my numbers reflected this too.

CHAPTER 13

LOVE WHAT YOU DO!

If you love what you do then success will follow. If you do not enjoy the selling process of making calls, presentations, getting rejected, losing deals, winning deals, then do not do it; find another profession. If you believe you need to stay in this profession or have to keep on selling, then keep on reading this book and pause on each and every word. Work constructively to re-focus your efforts and re-program your brain to become the Sales Superstar that you need to be right now. The results will be amazing!

Think for a moment about your personal life. What feelings do you have in those relationships where you truly love a person regardless of any shortcomings? What do you do to make it work? What amount of effort do you put in? Do you find yourself being more creative and exciting?

The old adage "You get what you put into a relationship" holds true in business. Stop doing the busy work that is taking time away from getting yourself where you need to be. Practice and preparation over and over again will program you to become that which you need to be. Repetition can only get you better than you are now. There may be one or two calls that go very poorly. HOWEVER, there will be many more on which you sound great, confident and believable. This will help turn you into a believer and lover of what you do. And yes, the results will reflect this. Your new passion and excitement for what you do will inspire others to come along for the ride!

Skills That Are Required

Chapter 14

Learn The Art Of Asking Intelligent Questions

Every profession is known for something special or unique that it does. Doctors ask questions when you go in for a checkup or when something is bothering you. As a patient you never question the doctor or feel intruded upon when the doctor asks you question after question. Why? The reason you feel it is okay for the doctor to ask you questions is because he is a professional who is trying to uncover what ails you and prescribe the appropriate solution. He needs information in order to do his job properly. The same is true with a dentist, accountant, or attorney.

As a Professional Sales Superstar you do the same thing. The Sales Superstar asks appropriate, professional questions to uncover the prospect's problem and determine whether (or in what way) his product or service can solve the problem. If there is a fit, then great. If not, the sales professional moves on to someone who can use his services. Be stingy with your time. Do not waste it where there is not a clear-cut fit. Move on to find your next true prospect... before your competitor does.

The sooner you realize that your job is to ask professional questions the sooner you will become successful.

CHAPTER 15

ASK HIGH GAIN, OPEN-ENDED QUESTIONS

These are questions that begin with the words Who, What, When, Where, Why, and How. Any question that cannot be answered with a "Yes" or "No" is high-gain, open-ended.

For example, "How long have you been using xyz product? What is it that you like about it? What is it that you do not like about it? What would you change or do differently?"

Why ask these types of questions instead of yes/no questions? Because "yes/no" answers lead you nowhere and absolutely kill the sales process. Also they tend to make the prospect feel as though he is being interrogated! That's NOT where you want to be.

Here is a great example of NOT making any head-way: *"Are you currently looking for a new vendor?"* "NO, GOODBYE!"

If you ask appropriate, open-ended questions you begin to build credibility, a relationship, and most importantly gain insight and knowledge into the prospect's mind.

What is holding you back? How well do you know your product or service? Why is the competition beating you? What do you need to do to turn your career around?

See Appendix A for some excellent high-gain, open–ended questions.

CHAPTER 16

BE A CONSULTATIVE SALES PROFESSIONAL

This means you are a consultant to the prospect and not a salesperson. I hate it when someone says, "Oh you are a salesman". If they say or even think that, then I am not doing my job. Your job is to ask intelligent questions while being fully prepared. Your job is to make the prospect feel as though you are there to truly help by discovering what the issues at hand are. What have they done to resolve them? What has worked or not worked and why? Unless you play the detective and consultant, you will not get the information that you need to be as effective as you possibly can or need to be. Just as important, if you do not ask appropriate questions and get the information YOU need, you may be dragging this "potential sale" along when it never WAS a potential sale! Again, do not waste your time. Your time is valuable and there isn't a lot of it. Get what you need to evaluate whether or not this is truly worth your investment. Then move along.

The best sales professionals are consultants. The sooner you are able to develop appropriate high-gain, open-ended sales questions for your prospects, the sooner you will start closing more business. You must show your prospects that you care about them and are focused on their needs rather than exclusively on your commission.

CHAPTER 17

UNDERSTAND THE INDUSTRY

If you are consulting in the paper industry, then read all the paper publications there are. If you are in the telecommunications industry read all the telecommunication magazines and so on. It is absolutely amazing: knowledge truly is what sells. I have seen completely terrible sales professionals make sales and be somewhat successful because they were knowledgeable about their industry.

The bottom-line is that without industry-appropriate knowledge your chances for success go down significantly. I was able to sell at a quota-breaking pace my whole career because of my sales skills and always knowing "Just enough to be dangerous". I was very aware of the industry I was in…what was happening, what affected it and what the news was in the industry. Make this an important priority for you too in your own industry.

The biggest obstacle to manage while you are gaining this industry knowledge is your time. Time management (discussed later in the book) is critical. Remember you get paid to sell, not to read textbooks all day. A quick way to stay abreast of industry and/or company information is to conduct a quick daily internet search for news on that topic.

CHAPTER 18

KNOW CURRENT EVENTS

Just as it is important to know what is happening in your particular industry, it is crucial to your success that you understand what is happening in the news locally, regionally, nationally, and across the globe. Business, economic, and world news issues all contribute to your success or lack of success. Read headlines, articles and anything of significance. Know what world events could affect your industry.

What would happen if you walked into a presentation without knowing that the prospect was recently acquired by or themselves purchased another firm? What would happen if you walked into a presentation and the person you were presenting to had just been passed over for a major promotion? What would happen if you walked into a presentation and did not know that your prospect's competition just had a major (positive or negative) article appearing in that day's *Wall Street Journal*?

YOU must be informed and stay abreast of the world around you!

CHAPTER 19

READ BUSINESS BOOKS

It is also important that you read general business books that fill your mind with knowledge. Knowledge truly is power. The knowledge gained from business books offers a different perspective from world or local news events. Read sales books, books on your industry, autobiographies of successful people in any industry, business books written by people such as Donald Trump, Lee Iacocca, Tony Robbins, etc.

Reading these books will contribute to your success. In my career, two books that made the biggest difference to my success were 1. *How to Win Friends and Influence People* by Dale Carnegie, and 2. Books by Richard Marcinko (the Rogue Warrior).

These books confirm everything I believe in and teach. Dale Carnegie books basically say *"Let people talk and you will learn something and they will probably like you"*. Marcinko books talk about preparation. In his books he stresses that no matter how well you prepare "Old Mr. Murphy of Murphy's Law" will always appear. In other words no sales call is ever the same and the prospect will always throw you a curve ball. This makes complete preparation crucial.

Read, listen, prepare, then repeat.

CHAPTER 20

QUALIFY, QUALIFY, AND QUALIFY

What separates the average from the truly great Superstar Sales Professionals? Truly great Superstars qualify their prospects better than anyone else. What is qualifying? Simply, it is asking appropriate questions at the appropriate time.

What Superstar Sales professionals understand is that their time is very important and that asking excellent qualifying questions not only improves their time management but also increases the time they will spend with prospects that are ready, willing and able to buy.

What are some standard qualifying questions that you could use immediately regardless of what you are selling? Below are some proven questions that are guaranteed to get your prospects talking while at the same time improve your credibility in the eyes of the prospect.

EXCELLENT QUALIFYING QUESTIONS:

Why are you using x?

How long have you been using x?

What specifically do you like about x?

What specifically do you not like about x or would like to see improved?

Who else in your company is involved with using x or is involved in the decision to use x?

How often do you use x?

How long have you been with the company?

How long have you been in your current role?

Was x in place before you took over this role?

Were you involved in the decision to purchase x for your company?

This is a sampling of some of the questions you could and should ask on every sales presentation. It is important to note that you only ask the prospect questions about himself and his company. Not once did you ask a question that pertained directly to your product or service. Why do you think that is important?

The reason this is important is because you are being a CONSULTANT. Consultants ask questions and gather information and they listen carefully. They do not talk about themselves. This approach works no matter what industry you are in. It is true that sooner or later you must talk about your product or service. **This will and should happen only after you have gathered enough information so you can tailor your presentation about those aspects of your product or service that are meaningful for or important to your prospect.**

Face it: there are a lot of benefits that you could talk about. Why not ask some questions and find out what is important and/or applicable to your prospect first? This way you can zero-in on speaking about and emphasizing those attributes that appeal to him most. Getting this information allows you to tailor your next questions and presentation to your company's strengths not weaknesses. Think of yourself as a doctor of selling.

As a doctor you must ask many questions before you can make an accurate diagnosis. Imagine going to a doctor who asked you no questions and simply wrote a prescription for you to fill and take! What kind of credibility would that doctor have in your eyes? How would you feel about taking that doctor's advice? Why would you take the medication when he does not know what ails you?

You wouldn't. You would look for other opinions. You would certainly expect any competent doctor to ask you questions BEFORE prescribing anything. There is no difference in sales. If you do not do enough consulting, your prospects will look for someone who will!

Be a stickler for qualifying and consulting.

CHAPTER 21

BUILD A SOLID, WELL-QUALIFIED PIPELINE.

Too many sales people build pipelines that are fictitious. In other words, they list 30 companies that are prospects when in reality only 1 or 2 may be true prospects.

What is a qualified prospect? No matter what line of business you are in, a qualified prospect is someone who has money to invest within a reasonable period of time (this will vary greatly depending on your product) and is very interested in investing in your product or service. Simple, isn't it? The typical sales person creates a pipeline of fairy dust. Theirs is a pipeline of people they've called or want to call rather than a list of people who have the money and inclination to invest in a solution (your solution) in the short term. Do NOT create a pipeline of fluff. It will waste your time and not make you any money.

Having a pipeline that is filled with fluff is easy to do. By not asking appropriate questions about timing, money, needs, etc, you will have a very full pipeline of truly unqualified prospects who will likely never buy anything from you. You need to shorten the pipeline to include prospects that are ready, willing and have the means and incentive to make a decision in the short term. How can you improve your pipeline?

TAKE THE FOLLOWING STEPS:

Be honest with yourself. Ask yourself, "What is needed to close this sale?" After you start filling in the blanks you will uncover how realistic it is to believe this prospect is a real prospect or a truly unqualified prospect. You will be able to tell whether the sale will close soon or whether you haven't asked enough hard-hitting questions to provide you the information you need.

Be extremely conservative. If you think a sale has a 95% chance of closing, report it as a 75% chance. Things happen; some of them predictable, others not predictable. Travel schedules, real authority to "ok" a sale, illness and vacation schedules all affect timing and closure.

Ask your prospects point blank. That's right. Ask your prospects if they see themselves moving forward with your product/services. Their answer will help you know with better certainty if your projections are correct. They know better than anyone whether this sale has ANY chance of closing. If it doesn't, they will tell you their objections and hesitations. What they say and do not say will be very revealing. This provides you with an opportunity to overcome these objections and to get back on track.

Use an internal checklist. Prepare a checklist of every possible thing that needs to be addressed in order for the sale to come in or close. Your checklist of questions might include: Am I speaking to all the right (or the true) decision makers? Does the prospect see the value of my product or service? Is my service right for the prospect or is my competition the right solution? What is the internal process to get this done when they say "yes, let's do it"? Does the contract need to go to legal for review? Is this sign-off person out of the country or out sick? When during the week or month are checks or P.O.'s issued?

It is extremely important to note that even though you think your product is the greatest it may not be right for this prospect's needs. The better you understand your product or service the sooner you will be able to sell to the right prospects.

Be true to yourself, and to your company. A fictitous pipeline hurts the company and you.

CHAPTER 22

TIME MANAGEMENT

Truly understand how you spend your day. If you work 40 hours per week, how many hours are actually being spent contacting prospects and how many hours are actually spent speaking to them? How much time are you spending "researching" the prospect before you call to qualify them? Is your time spent on "busy" work that will not reap financial rewards? Are you doing things that take time away from speaking to potential clients (like pushing paper? Organizing? Looking for a stray piece of paper somewhere?) My research shows that sales people spend less than one hour a day speaking with decision makers. That leaves a lot of time for other activities. That's a lot of wasted time.

So how do Sales Superstars manage their time?

First, they make sure that the largest possible percentage of time every day is spent talking to decision makers who can invest in their products and services. Second, they make sure that their appointments are in similar locations and not scattered across the map. This rule does not apply if you are selling a product or service that is a big-ticket item with few prospects. However, if you are selling in a region where thousands of prospects are close to each other geographically, make sure you schedule many meetings in a similar area.

What about paperwork and administrative duties?

Do all administrative tasks before or after hours. Your manager will give you plenty of leeway if your numbers are great but will be an absolute pain in the ass if your numbers are poor and your paperwork is late. Produce big numbers, worry about the paperwork later.

Invest your time wisely. This is the only thing you can truly control. Proper time management is your biggest ally. If misused, it is your biggest enemy.

CHAPTER 23

PRACTICE, PRACTICE, PRACTICE -

AND THEN PRACTICE SOME MORE

The average sales person does not prepare for sales presentations and/or telephone calls. The average sales person wings it! Why do professional athletes go to spring training or hire coaches to help them? Aren't they already professionals? Have they already achieved superstar status?

The answer is "yes, they are already stars. But true professionals practice and practice. You MUST practice to maintain and improve no matter what your profession. Focus on those areas that need work and find ways to improve them. When you speak, are you smiling or frowning? Are you using your hands too much when speaking and causing an annoying distraction? Are you constantly interrupting others when they are speaking?

Listed below are some superstar keys to practice:

Rehearse exactly what you want to say for your introduction. The introduction sets the tone for the entire meeting. The Superstar's introduction addresses many keys for success including: outlining the goals of the meeting, outlining what will be addressed and accomplished and possible next steps.

Predict what the prospect's key objections will be and address these objections before they are raised by the prospect. If you can master this one concept, your closing percentages will go up considerably.

For example, you know or feel that the prospect is going to object to the fact that your product or service is new to the marketplace and has no track record. This is the objection but the real objection to the prospect is not the newness of the product but his feeling that he might get burned or a buy a lemon.

How do you make this feeling go away? That's right, use proof. As you are going through your presentation address this feeling by stating that all of your clients or current prospects use your product or service for a trial period. The trial period allows the user to get used to using the product while at the same time taking away his fear of making a bad decision. If you are unable to allow trials then use proof (customer testimonials, references). Do not wait for the objection to hit you square in the face. If you do, you will begin to get defensive and you may start backpedaling and start to sound like a salesperson instead of a sales consultant.

Practice good habits. Practice makes perfect.

CHAPTER 24

KAZIEN: CONTINUAL IMPROVEMENT

Kaizen means continual improvement. The only way to get better is through constant scrutiny and evaluation of what you are doing right and wrong. This is what professionals do. Professionals work on these things when no one is watching.

No matter what your profession you must continually learn, practice, make mistakes, understand what went right and wrong and start again. Look at any profession: doctors, lawyers, scientists, financial planners, corporate executives, professional athletes, actors. Why do professional athletes spend an enormous amount of time watching game films? Why do actors rehearse constantly? Why do doctors and other professionals go through years and years of training? Because if you want to be a professional and get paid like one you must act like one. Always be improving.

As I am writing this the New England Patriots just won their 20th straight football game. Even so, their coach starts off every meeting with "Great job, but this is what we need to do to get better". As a rule always take five minutes after every presentation and figure out what went right and wrong and make sure you make the necessary adjustments for your next call.

CHAPTER 25

EDUCATION

No matter where you stand in relation to others at your company (1st in sales performance or last) make sure you continually improve your sales skills via seminars, books, and courses. Read books like this one, listen to audiotapes, watch videos and CDs, go on the road with the best sales people, videotape or audiotape yourself and see what you sound and look like.

Invest in yourself especially when you think you are too busy. This investment will pay dividends in ways you cannot foresee. The knowledge you gain will help you garner higher sales numbers and improve your understanding of the world around you.

Currently, I estimate that I have read close to 90% of the sales books published and have attended 50% of the sales training seminars in existence. Even though I have been selling professionally at the highest level for over 20 years I still seek out additional training every day. Why? Professionals never stop learning.

The bottom line: School is never out.

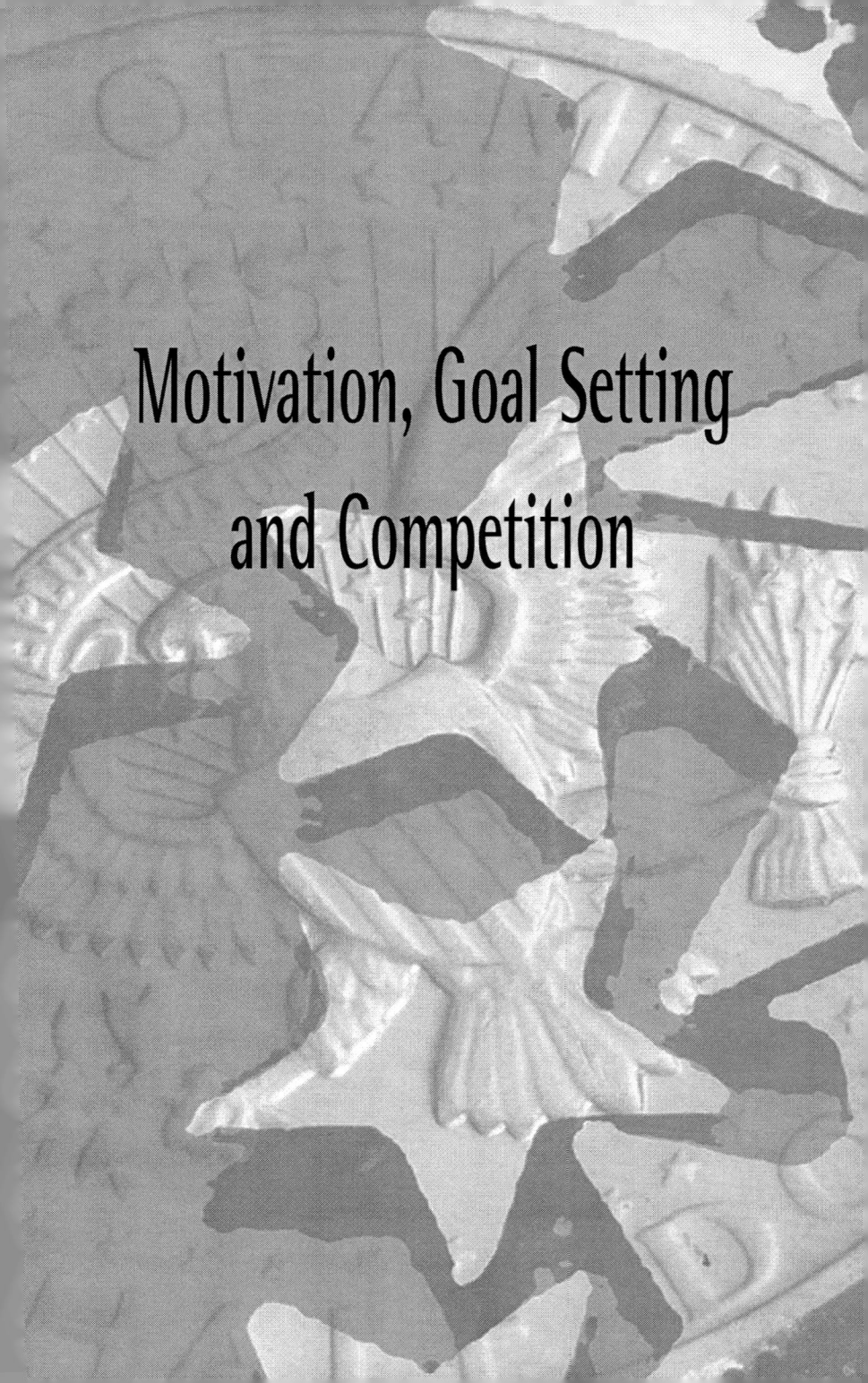

Motivation, Goal Setting and Competition

CHAPTER 26

MAKE THE CALLS

Many sales people never make enough calls. The old expression that sales is a numbers game is so very true. You have to make calls to succeed. Eventually you may get to a point where the only calls you are making are referral calls (the best way to succeed). Until then you need to dial for dollars using a strategic game plan.

What is the right number of calls to make? That is 100% up to you and your abilities. Figure out how many calls it takes you to get a qualified lead, and then figure out how many leads it takes to get one sale. That's when you will have your answer.

A brief example: If it takes 100 calls to get one lead, and it takes five leads to close one sale, then you need to make 500 calls to close one deal. If your quota is three deals per month then you need to make 1,500 calls monthly.

If you improve your selling skills and are able to make only 50 calls to get one lead and only need three leads to close a deal, then you need to make 150 calls to close a deal and only need to make 450 calls monthly to meet your quota.

It's purely a numbers game. But make sure your skills are always improving. As you can see from the above example with improved skills you may be able to make 60-80% fewer calls and still hit your goals.

One year I closed 99 straight deals without losing a sale and closed 175 out of 182 opportunities for the year. I made the calls but more importantly I knew what I was doing.

CHAPTER 27

STRATEGIC SELLING

My company Strategic Sales Closers provides workshops on this topic. Strategic Selling is what you need to do in order to be successful. What is strategic selling?

Strategic Selling is the process of carefully analyzing your territory, prospects, competition, your product or services, yourself, your resources, your company's competitive strength, weakness, industry standing, your prospect's likes and dislikes, wants versus needs, past history, current viewpoint, future projections and so on.

In other words, Strategic Selling is a collection of every possible important piece of information and strategy that will either win or lose the deal for you. The best strategic sales professionals are the top selling sales professionals.

As a professional you must gather and use a tremendous amount of information at key strategic moments. Your ability to use the information appropriately at key moments will be the difference between winning and losing. Everything in this book will help you reach the highest levels of strategic selling.

It is up to you. You must put in the time and work to get the results you desire. Your first step to achieving this result is to make sure you believe in your product or service and your company. If you can reach this first goal everything else will be much easier.

Work! Do not go through the motions.

CHAPTER 28

GOAL SETTING

This is one of the most crucial parts of being successful. Without goals you aimlessly flounder every day not knowing if you are successful or not.

What are goals? Goals are tangible numbers. In other words, if your goal is to make one sale, you need to break down the number of calls it takes to get through to a decision maker, the number of decision makers it takes to get a meeting, the number of meetings it takes to get a sale. This is basic stuff but unless you are using this formula you are not maximizing your potential.

I find it very helpful to set timetables with each goal. This helps to reach the desired goal and also pushes you toward the goal. For example, every morning my goal might be to contact 25 companies to see if they will have an interest in my professional services. The time that I set is from 8 – 10 A.M. Therefore, I have two hours to reach my goals, then I move on to my next goals. I do not go over the time limit and I make sure I reach my goals.

You need to be very strict with your time. Your time is the most crucial resource you have as a professional salesperson. Set goals that are achievable yet make you reach for the sky.

On a final note, if you want to become a superstar in your company, take the quota number that has been given to you and multiply it by FIVE. Then work the numbers that you need to do (calls, meetings, sales) and try to do it. This technique works. Remember the sales quota your manager sets for you is just a number. Why settle for his number.

By the way, if you only reach 50% of your larger number you are still at 250% of quota for the year. Those are super-star numbers!

Set a target and do not stop until you reach it!

CHAPTER 29

MOTIVATION

What motivates you? Money, recognition, security, being part of a team?

On a sheet of paper write exactly what gets you motivated or excited. Is it money? Is it being number one in your company? Is it being recognized among your peers? Is it being part of a team? Is it security in your job? Is it the safety of having a job? Is it winning a sales contest? Is it out-producing someone you work with?

Use this information to help you get and stay motivated daily. Take this information and let your manager know. It will make his job easier and will translate into better performance by you. Your better performance will yield for you the things that motivate you.

Your motivation is what drives you to succeed. I could train you with every possible way to close deals. Unless you are motivated and excited about what you do, training you would be a waste of time. That is why the most important step to becoming a Sales Superstar is choosing the right product and company for you to represent. It will become very difficult for you to stay motivated if you do not believe in the product or service you represent or if you find it boring.

If you are highly motivated the sky is the limit.

CHAPTER 30

DO NOT BE AFRAID TO LOSE

Losing is what makes us stronger, better, and tougher.

Make sure you always learn and understand why you lost the deal. Was it a bad fit? Did the prospect not like you? Was your product at fault? Was there a reason outside of your control? Did you do a poor job managing the process? Were you speaking to the wrong level?

Losing is the greatest ally of the Superstar Sales Professional. That's right. Losing is the greatest ally of the Superstar Sales Professional. Sales Superstars learn more from losing than they do from winning. Losing makes Sales Superstars smarter and stronger. It helps to build character, helps the Superstar to handle adversity better. Sales Superstars know that if they have truly learned from losing, it has made them in to champions. If you are able to take all the positives from losing, then you can end up being more successful than you ever imagined.

I know because I have lost countless times. But at the end of the day the only thing that matters (in sales) is what your numbers are. Your manager does not care that you lost 100 times; he just wants to know your sales numbers are where they need to be. Remember: A Hall of Fame baseball player hits 300. That means he fails 7 out of 10 times at bat! And he's still in the Hall of Fame! Amazing!

Losing is what makes you great as long as you learn from it. But do not make a habit of it!

CHAPTER 31

COMPETITION

Know the competition better than they know themselves. We live in an age of incredible access to information. The Internet provides a wealth of knowledge with the click of the mouse. It is inexcusable to go into a sales presentation and not know what your competition is saying about you, or how much they typically quote, what their strengths and weaknesses are, why they win and lose, who the sales rep is, and finally who their customers are.

Your competition is there to make you better. Because their job is to beat you, it becomes your job to understand them better than they understand themselves. Many years ago I invested countless hours and put together a 200-page book report on my competitors. This report showed my prospects and me exactly what the facts were and what the fiction was. This report allowed me to become the #1 producing sales professional for a number of years. This report gave me instant credibility because I knew the competition inside and out! I knew what they had and didn't have; I knew what they were offering and why. I knew what they were saying about my product...and I was able to diffuse that "objection" before it even became an issue! My reputation as an expert and as someone with a tremendous amount of value to my clients quickly spread to other prospects. This yielded more referrals and sales than I had ever dreamed possible.

When I think of how competition can make you better I always think of the 1992 Summer Olympics and a lesser-known story. At the 1992 Summer Games American swimmer Jeff Rouse placed second in the backstroke swim meet, winning the silver medal. He lost by less than one second to Canadian swimmer, Mark Tewksbury. As the Canadian National Anthem was being played, Rouse was upset but very determined never to lose again.

Over the next four years he dedicated himself to winning the gold in 1996. At the 1996 games he won the gold medal with a winning margin of more than one second. The interesting part of the story is that immediately after the race he called Tewksbury (Tewksbury did not compete that year) to **thank him** for helping to motivate him and perform at his highest level.

Master your competition so you can become a true ally to your prospects. Your competition will make you better and will go a long way in helping you to become a Sales Superstar. Turn the competition into a motivating positive force. Thank them for making you better (This is especially easy to do when you are winning all the deals).

CHAPTER 32

ETHICS

Ethics – def. the story of right versus wrong, in actions, personal standards of right versus wrong, standards of conduct adopted by professionals.

Never compromise. Always ask yourself: "Is this right or wrong"? Then decide what to do.

My two favorite quotes regarding ethics follow. Read these quotes over and over and use them whenever you are faced with a crucial decision that may compromise your morals and ethics.

THE MAN IN THE GLASS

When you get what you want in your struggle for self
And the World makes you king for a day
Just go the mirror and look at yourself
And see what the man has to say
For it isn't your father or mother or wife
Whose judgment upon you must pass
The fellow whose verdict counts most in your life
Is the one staring back from the glass.
Some people might think you a straight–shootin' chum
And call you a wonderful guy,
But the man in the glass says you're only a bum
If you can't look him straight in the eye.
He's the fellow to please, never mind all the rest,

For he's with you clear up to the end.
And you've passed your most dangerous, difficult test.
If the man in the glass is your friend.
You may fool the whole world down the pathway of
Life and get pats on your back as you pass,
But you will find reward will be heartaches and tears
If you've cheated the man in the glass.

—By Dale Wimbrow.

Prefer a loss to a dishonest gain.
The one brings pain at the moment;
the other for all time.
—Chilon

CHAPTER 33

DO NOT WORRY ABOUT CLOSING THE DEAL

Every sales book ever written talks about how to close and what to say and spells out different closing techniques.

What a bunch of nonsense. Closing the deal is nothing more than two parties agreeing to move forward. When you decide to go out to dinner with friends do you use closing techniques? Of course not, you discuss where everyone wants to go then discuss the pros and cons and then come up with the choice that most people agree on.

Closing is nothing more than the natural outcome of two or more parties doing what should come next. If you are a true professional, the prospect will already know long in advance what the next steps are and ask you for the contract to get signed.

There should be no suspense in closing. If you have any anxiety about this step then maybe you should change the name to "NEXT LOGICAL STEPS". Then simply ask the prospect *"Based on the information we just covered what do you think?"* Or *"Do you see yourself moving forward in the process?"*

If you are acting like a professional Sales Superstar the act of closing the deal will be as natural as walking. Just make sure that when you trip, you pick yourself up and keep on walking.

SUMMARY AND CONCLUSION

This book is designed to help you achieve Superstar Selling Greatness. You **MUST WORK** at becoming great. This means many setbacks along the way. Make sure you learn from each and every lost sale. Make sure you never lose a positive outlook and make sure you never ever give up.

Early in my career I lost sales for six straight months to competition before finally breaking through. I then spent the next six years beating the pants off this competitor. If I had not lost as many times as I did initially, then I never would have worked as hard as I did and realized my incredible potential. Losing is not fun. Working hard and then achieving greatness is a great feeling.

I hope this book will help you achieve all of your goals. Please refer back to it often as a reminder of what Sales Superstars do daily and what you can do now to get to Sales Superstar status.

Best of Luck and Good Selling.
Michael Leppo
President
Strategic Sales Closers
www.strategicsalesclosers.com
609-620-1768

APPENDIX A

HIGH GAIN, OPEN–ENDED QUESTIONS
(QUESTIONS ARE TO SALES PROFESSIONALS WHAT A HAMMER IS TO A CARPENTER).

Open-ended questions start with the words Who, What, Where, When, Why, and How.

Some questions listed below should be very similar. They were designed so that you would be able to find questions that best match your personality and style.

WHO QUESTIONS

1. Who will be involved in the decision–making process?
2. Who will be using the product or service?
3. Who needs to sign off on this project?
4. Who is on the selection committee?
5. Who is the key person in making this decision?
6. Who do you think I need to convince?

Questions # 5 and 6 would be asked at the appropriate time and if you feel you have an excellent relationship with the prospect.

WHAT QUESTIONS

1. What do you think of what you have just seen or heard (Very important question to gauge if you are winning or losing based on their response)?
2. What do you feel are the three most important features this product or service must have?
3. What are some features you would like to have?
4. What is your timetable for making a decision?
5. What obstacles do you see standing in the way of moving forward with this project?
6. What is your past experience with ABC's product or service?
7. What has been your experience with your current product?
8. What feedback have you been getting from the users of your current product (problems, good or bad)?
9. What are your company's plans for use of this product or service?
10. What do you need from me in order to make a decision?
11. What do you need to see from me in order to make a decision?
12. What problems have you been having with your current service?
13. What will you base your decision on?
14. What do you currently like, dislike, or would like to see improved in your current product?

WHERE QUESTIONS

1. Where are the different offices located that will use this product or service?
2. Where are decision makers #1, 2 and 3 located?
3. Where do you see this product or service impacting your business in the greatest manner?
4. Where have you seen the greatest need for this product or service?
5. Where would you like training to occur?
6. Where do you foresee using this product as your company grows during the next 1-3 years?
7. Where does this product fit into your strategic plan?

WHEN QUESTIONS

1. When is the best time for me to reach you?
2. When would you like to meet? (You could provide the prospect with a choice – is Monday at 2 or Tuesday at 3 better for you?).
3. When will you be able to let me know if you will be moving forward?
4. When will the key decision maker be back in town?
5. When does your current contract expire?
6. When did you sign with ABC?
7. When are vendors able to submit bids?
8. When do you want this product installed or service to begin?
9. When are other vendors coming in to present?
10. When will your budget be ready?
11. When could you accept delivery?

Why Questions

1. Why is your company using ABC's product or service?
2. Why is your company considering switching?
3. Why did you contact my company? (How did you hear about my company and what caught your attention?)

How Questions

1. How often do you use the product or service?
2. How does the internal decision making process work at your company?
3. How many other vendors are bidding on this project?
4. How do you envision implementing this product or service?

APPENDIX B

POWER WORDS

Power words are words that convey confidence and assume that a prospect WILL do business with you. The list below shows some of the words you should use that will help you instill confidence in your prospects so they will select your company's products or services.

Power Words That Show Confidence	*Words That Show Lack of Conviction*
Yes	Maybe, Might
Will	Possibly, Could
Definitely	Not Sure, May
Absolutely	We have never done that
What ever it takes	It is not my department or job
Just tell me what you need	I cannot be bothered with that at this time
I am 100% confident	It looks like it may work
You are right	You are wrong

APPENDIX C

TOP MOTIVATIONAL QUOTES

"All things are difficult before they are easy"
—John Norley

"Adversity reveals genius, prosperity conceals it".
—Horace

"The price of greatness is responsibility".
—Winston Churchill

"Destiny is not a matter of chance, it is a matter of choice".
—Unknown

"People forget how fast you did a job —
but they remember how well you did it".
—Howard W. Newton

"Accept the challenges, so that you may
feel the exhilaration of victory".
—General George S. Patton

"The difference between ordinary
and extraordinary is that little extra".
—Unknown

"Luck is what happens when preparation
meets opportunity".
—Elmer Letterman

"Success is simply a matter of luck. Ask any failure"
—Unknown

"Doubt whom you will, but never yourself".
—Unknown

"The people who get on in this world are the people who get up and look for the circumstances they want, and, if they can't find them, make them".
—George Bernard Shaw

"Chance favors the prepared mind".
—Louis Pasteur

"You will become as small as your controlling desire; as great as your dominant aspiration".
—James Allen

"Genius is the ability to reduce the complicated to the simple".
—C.W. Ceran

"Things may come to those who wait, but only the things left by those who hustle".
—Abraham Lincoln

Don't wait for your ship to come in, swim out to it".
—Unknown

The man who believes he can do something is probably right, and so is the man who believes he can't".
—Unknown

"Stop talking, start listening".
—Michael Leppo

"When nothing seems to help, I go and look
at a stonecutter hammering away at his rock
perhaps a hundred times without as much
as a crack showing in it. Yet at the hundred and
first blow it will split in two, and I know it was
not that blow that did it – but all that had gone before".
–Jacob RIIS
(This is one of my all time favorites
and one I read daily to keep me going.)

"Yesterday is a cancelled check; tomorrow is a promissory
note; today is the only cash you have – so spend it wisely".
–Kay Lyons

"Winning is not a something thing; it's an all the time thing.
You don't win once in a while, you don't do things right
once in a while, you do them right all the time. Winning is a
habit. Unfortunately, so is losing."
–Vincent Lombardi

"He who believes is strong; he who doubts is weak.
Strong convictions precede great actions."
–J.F. Clarke

"Every job is a self-portrait of the person who did it.
Autograph your work with excellence."
–Unknown

APPENDIX D

PROFESSIONAL RESOURCES

Listed below are a few professional references. I limited the list to sources that really will make a positive difference to you and not waste your time.

Books by Richard Marcinko - His books are not sales books but rather semi-autobiographical stories of his days in the Navy Seals. These books impart an excellent lesson. The lesson of preparation. **Think of selling as preparing for battle then read his books.**

Dale Carnegie – *How To Win Friends and Influence People.* All time classic of how to communicate with others. A must read.

Selling Magazine – www.selling.com. This is an excellent source of selling information.

Books, Tapes, Sales Training, and *Coaching/Mentoring from Michael Leppo and Strategic Sales Closers.* I believe that I am the World's Greatest Sales Person, Trainer, and Coach. Get your company to hire me and my company to make you and your fellow Sales Professionals Sales Superstars.

HOW TO INVEST IN ADDITIONAL COPIES

STRATEGIC SALES CLOSERS
THE SALES SUPERSTAR BIBLE
EVERYTHING YOU NEED TO KNOW TO BE THE
TOP PRODUCING SALES PROFESSIONAL IN YOUR COMPANY

# Of books	Cost per book
1–100	$13.95
101–500	$12.75
501–1,000	$11.65
1001–10,000	$10.55
10,000+	Call or email for a quote

To order contact:

Strategic Sales Closers
10 Dustin Drive
Lawrenceville, NJ. 08648
Phone: 609-620-1768

email: info@strategicsalesclosers.com

Use the above contact information to inquire about consulting and training services for your company.

NOTES

NOTES

ABOUT THE AUTHOR

Michael Leppo is widely known as the World's greatest Sales Professional, Sales Trainer, and Motivational Sales Expert. Mr. Leppo is the President and Founder of Strategic Sales Closers (SSC) a leading Sales Consulting company specializing in Sales Training, consulting, and coaching. SSC is designed to create superstar performers who will average a minimum of 150% of quota year in and year out. Listed below are some of Mr. Leppo's achievements:

- Trained over 1,000 sales professionals on how to become a superstar sales performer.
- Lifetime sales record of 500% of quota (20 years).
- Closed over 15,000 deals ranging in size from $1 to $5M with cycle times of 1 minute to three years.
- Sold over 1,000 products and services including office equipment, financial software, professional services, financial consulting, negotiating and motivational services, public speaking, marketing, b-to-b auction services, and many others.
- Won most outstanding sales professional 13 times.
- Amazing ability to train sales professionals on how to close more business no matter what their product or service is.
- Highly trained motivational speaker, marketing and negotiation expert.
- Regarded by many as having the greatest sales mind in the country.

Mr. Leppo is married and has two children. He lives in Lawrenceville, New Jersey.